Rescue service

Tessa Krailing

Nelson

WELLINGTON SQUARE

Contents

Who will save Sing-Sing?

Rocky and Max often went to see Mr Keeping.
Mr Keeping had lots of animals and Rocky liked to go and see them.
Max was kept on a lead so that he didn't chase the animals and frighten them.
Max didn't like being on a lead and one day he got away.
What a lot of trouble there was when that happened!

Rocky was talking to Mr Keeping about one of his new animals.
Max was sitting quietly by his side.
He was sitting quietly until he saw the kitten on top of the fence!
Rocky wasn't holding the lead very tightly and suddenly Max jumped up.
The lead slipped out of Rocky's hand and the dog ran away.
Max ran over to the kitten barking loudly.
The kitten gave a screech and ran up a tree.

Max sat under the tree barking at the kitten.
Mrs Valentine had heard the noise and
she came into Mr Keeping's garden.
She saw her kitten, Sing-Sing, up the tree.
She ran over to Max.
'Go away, you horrible dog!' she shouted.
'My poor little kitten!
Please will somebody rescue my poor
little Sing-Sing.'

'Max! Come here! Here, boy, here!' called Rocky.
Max gave a few more barks, then went over to Rocky.
Rocky grabbed his lead and held it tightly.
He looked at Sing-Sing up the tree.
'I'd rescue her myself but she's climbed too high.
I got stuck up a tree when I went to get
Wing Chan's dragon kite.'
'I'll call the fire brigade,' said Mrs Valentine.
'I don't think the fire brigade will come,'
said Mr Keeping.
'They'll wait to see if Sing-Sing will come
down by herself.'
'But she's only a kitten,' said Mrs Valentine,
'and the tree is so high!'

They looked up at the little kitten in the tree.
She looked very frightened.
'The branch she is on is so thin,' cried
Mrs Valentine.
'It might break! We must do something!'
'I'll call the RSPCA and see if they
can do anything,' said Mr Keeping.
He went inside his house to call the RSPCA.

A few minutes later, Mr Keeping came back.
'What did they say?' asked Mrs Valentine.
'They're sending someone over,' said Mr Keeping.
'They usually wait forty-eight hours to see if
a cat will come down by itself.
I told them that I didn't think Sing-Sing could
get down by herself.
I said the tree was very high and she was only
a little kitten.'
'Oh, I do hope they get here quickly,'
said Mrs Valentine.

Rescue!

It wasn't long before the RSPCA man came.
'I think you're right,' he said to Mr Keeping.
'I don't think the kitten can get down by herself.
She's too young and that tree is very high.'
'Can you get her down?' asked Mrs Valentine.
'I don't think so,' he said.
'We need the special sort of ladder that the
fire brigade has. I'd better give them a call.
They'll come out if they know the RSPCA
can't do anything.'

The fire brigade came quickly.
Fireman Salter looked at Sing-Sing high
up in the tree.
'How did she get up there?' he asked.
'That horrible dog chased her up that big tree.
Please get her down,' said Mrs Valentine.

Fireman Salter got a special ladder.
It was very long.
He put it up against the tree and began to
climb, slowly and carefully.
'That looks dangerous,' said Rocky.
'Yes,' said the RSPCA man.
'If it's really dangerous the fire brigade come.
They know what they're doing.'

When Fireman Salter got to the top of the ladder,
he reached out for Sing-Sing.
The kitten backed away and hissed at the fireman.
'Keep still, you stupid kitten,' said Fireman Salter.
'I'm trying to rescue you!'
He made a grab for Sing-Sing and
caught hold of her.

The fireman tucked Sing-Sing under his arm and climbed carefully down the ladder.
'Here she is,' he said to Mrs Valentine.
'Safe and sound.'
'Oh my poor little kitten,' said Mrs Valentine.
'That horrible dog should be locked up,'
she said to Rocky.

'Max loves chasing cats,' said Rocky
to the fireman.
'I'll have to keep him locked up.'
'All dogs love chasing cats,' said Fireman Salter.
'You can't keep them locked up for ever.'
'Thanks for coming,' said Rocky.
'That's OK,' said Fireman Salter.
'It's all part of the job.'

Rocky looked at the fire engine.
It was new and red and gleaming.
He said, 'NOW I know what I want to be when
I grow up. I want to be a fireman.'
When the fire engine had gone, Rocky took
Max back home.
'You're a bad dog, Max,' said Rocky.
'You know you shouldn't chase cats.
You'll have to stay in all day.'
Max felt very sorry for himself.

Fire!

When Rocky's Mum came home from work,
he told her about the fire brigade.
'When I grow up I'm going to be a fireman.
Then I can ride on the fire engine.'
'That can be a dangerous job,' said his Mum.
'It isn't just riding on fire engines, you know.'

When Rocky went to sleep that night he had
a dream about fire engines.
Something cold and wet touched his face.
He was sure it was a fire hose.
Then he woke up and found it was Max's nose.

'What's wrong, Max?
Did you hear something?'
Rocky sat up in bed. He sniffed.
'I can smell smoke!' he said.
'Something's on fire!
Where's the smoke coming from?
Quick, Max! Let's go and wake Mum, then
we'll look outside.'
Rocky jumped out of bed and ran into
his Mum's room.
She was already up because she had smelled
the smoke as well.

When Rocky and his Mum went outside there were lots of other people about.
Rocky ran down the street.
'Look, Mum! It's Mrs Valentine's house!
It's on fire!'
Mr Keeping came over and told Rocky to stand back.
'I've called the fire brigade and an ambulance.
They should be here any minute.'

Suddenly, Rocky saw Mrs Valentine at the window.
'Oh, look!' he shouted, pointing to
an upstairs window.
'There's Mrs Valentine. She must have woken up!'
'Should we smash the front window?' asked Rocky.
'No!' said Mr Keeping. 'We mustn't do that!
It will make the fire much bigger.'

Soon the fire engine's siren could be heard.
It pulled up outside Mrs Valentine's house.
The firemen jumped out.
'How many people inside?' asked Fireman Salter.
'As far as I know there's only Mrs Valentine,'
said Rocky's Mum.
'Right,' said the fireman.
He looked around quickly.
'This is a bad one, lads,' he said to
the other firemen.
'Smoke masks on to keep the smoke out!'

Fireman Salter climbed up to rescue Mrs Valentine.
She was very frightened.
She didn't want to stay in the house but
she didn't want to climb down the ladder!
Fireman Salter had to carry her down.
The ambulance men were waiting with a stretcher and
they quickly took her to hospital.

Saved again

Rocky watched the ambulance drive away.
'Will she be all right?' he asked.
'All that smoke will have made her ill,'
said Fireman Salter, 'but she'll be
OK in hospital.'

Suddenly, Max started to bark.
'What's wrong, Max?' said Rocky.
Then Rocky saw why Max was barking.
'Look!' he shouted. 'There's Mrs Valentine's
kitten on the roof.'

The fire engine was just about to leave.
Rocky ran over to Fireman Salter.
'Look,' he said, pointing to the roof.
'Sing-Sing is stuck on the roof.
Mrs Valentine loves that kitten.
She'll be very upset if we don't rescue it.'

‘Here we go again,’ said Fireman Salter.
‘Second time today I’ve had to rescue that kitten.
I hope she doesn’t hiss at me this time.’
Fireman Salter put the ladder up against
the house.
He climbed up to the roof.
He reached out to get the kitten.
Sing-Sing didn’t hiss.
She wanted to be rescued because she
was very frightened.
She let the fireman pick her up and
carry her down the ladder.

'Here's the kitten,' said Fireman Salter.
'Can someone look after her?
Mrs Valentine may be in hospital for
a week or two.'
'I'll look after her,' said Rocky.
'Poor Sing-Sing, she's had a fright.
Max will have to be good.
After all, he did save her life.'

The next day Rocky talked to Max before
he went to school.
'Now, Max, you have to be a good dog.
You must leave Sing-Sing alone.
No chasing her, OK?'

Sing-Sing watched Max all the time.
She still didn't trust him.
But Max was being a good dog.
He didn't chase the cat, but he would
have liked to!
Still, she wasn't such a bad cat.

When Rocky came home from school,
Fireman Salter was waiting for him.
'Would you like to come with me to see
Mrs Valentine?' he asked.
'Yes, please,' said Rocky.

Mrs Valentine was looking much better.
'What happened to Sing-Sing?' she asked.
'She's quite safe,' said Rocky.
'Someone's looking after her.'
He didn't tell her the someone was Max!

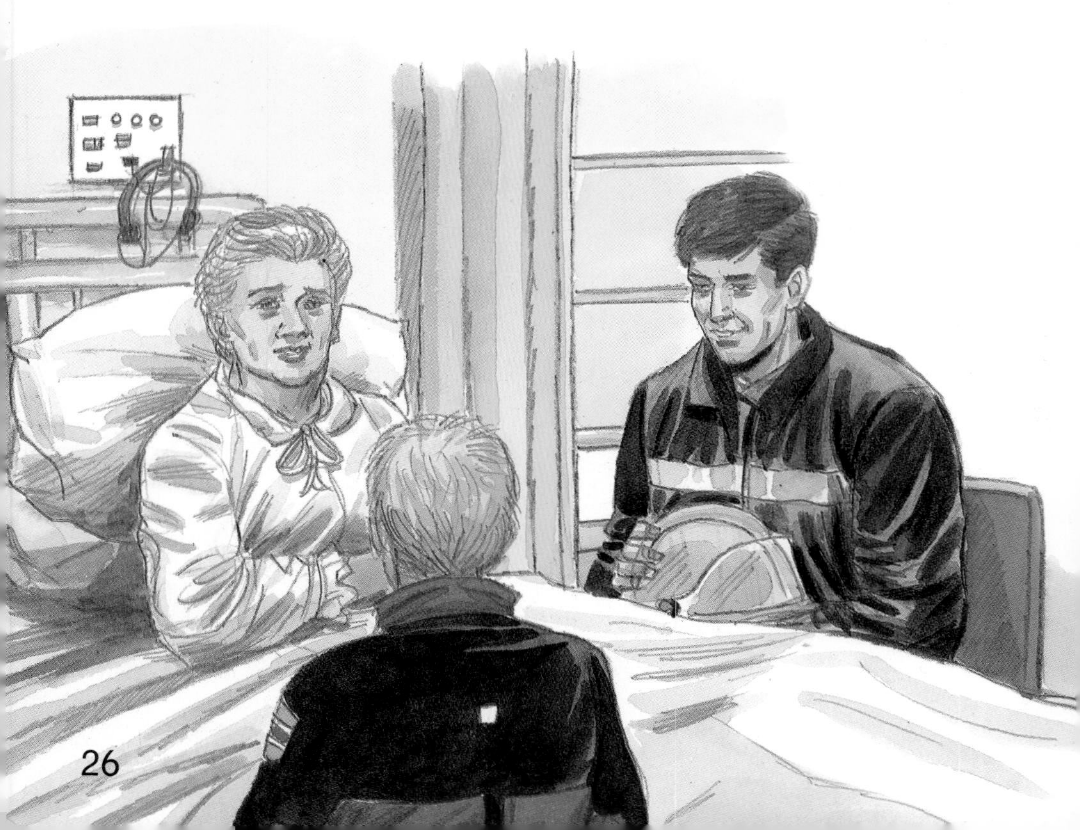

Rocky and Fireman Salter left the hospital.
'You said you wanted to be a fireman,'
said Fireman Salter.
'Would you like to come and look at the station?
Then you can see what it's all about.'
'Oh, yes, please,' said Rocky.

Fireman Salter drove to the fire station in his car.
He showed Rocky all around the fire station.
'We call the fire engines "pumps",' he told Rocky.
Suddenly there was a loud noise.
'That's the alarm,' said the fireman.
'One of the pumps has been called out.
You'll have to go home now, Rocky.'

Rocky was on his way home when the fire
engine passed him.
The siren made a loud noise and the light flashed.
Everyone on the road got out of the way.
The engine screeched round the corner.
Rocky ran after it to see what was happening.
He saw the fire engine stop at the end
of Waterloo Road.
There had been a road accident.
A man was trapped in his lorry.

The accident

The man wasn't badly hurt but he couldn't get out of the lorry.
'Don't worry,' said Fireman Salter.
'We'll soon have you out.'

The firemen had brought special gear.
It was gear for cutting through metal.
They cut through the door of the lorry and soon they rescued the man.

‘I thought firemen only put out fires,’
said Rocky to Fireman Salter.
‘But they have to do other things as well.
Like rescuing cats when they get stuck and
helping people in accidents.’
‘That’s right,’ said Fireman Salter.
‘We’re a rescue service.
Do you still want to be a fireman?’
‘I think so,’ said Rocky.
‘Yes, I want to be part of the rescue service.’
‘Would you like to try on my helmet?’ asked
Fireman Salter.
Rocky thought that was a great idea.
The fireman gave him the helmet and Rocky
put it on.
‘One day you might have one of your own,’ said
the fireman.
Rocky gave the fireman back his helmet and
went home.
He couldn’t wait to grow up so that he could be
a real fireman!

When Mrs Valentine came out of hospital,
Rocky's Mum asked her to come for a cup of tea.
She was very surprised to see Sing-Sing and
Max sitting together in the garden.
'They don't play together,' said Rocky,
'but Max doesn't chase her any more.'

Mrs Valentine bought a present for Rocky.
She gave him a small fire engine.
It was red and gleaming, just like a real engine.
Rocky played with the small engine and thought about the day when he would ride on a real one!